ISBN: 9798397473811

for someone brave

structured chaos

cheers

"floored" and "destination unknown" first appeared in *Flights*; "incorrect haiku" on *Troutswirl – The Haiku Foundation Blog*; "underaged" in *Versification*; "footprints" in *Fragments* (Fragmented Lines); "wrecking ball" in *Failed Haiku*; "keep yr photos," "the search" and "The Ballad of the Newsman" in *BlazeVOX*; "The Queen of Heart" in Cephalopress's *Ink Sac*; "worldview" in *Otherwise Engaged*; "construction work" in *Lotus-eater*; "low hanging fruit" and "undaunted gull" in *White Enso*; "Death in the City" in *Unlikely Stories Mark V*; "thrown from the nest" in *The Crank*; "Cockroaches find each other sexy" in *creatures*; "20/20s vision" in *Lune: The Journal of Literary Misrule*; "The Towers of London" and "the morning dew" in *The Journal of Wild Culture*; "esca(r)pe(ment)" in *A Spot of Writing*; "things to ban" in *Sein und Werden* (and in Chinese by *Poetry Lab Shanghai*); "the herd" in *Seppuku*; "landless bird" in *Heliosparrow*; "unnamed" in *CONSCIÒ*; "silent disco" in *Under the Bashō*; "becoming criminal" in *Rise Up Review*; "the wrong side of the law" in Coin-Operated Press's *Blackout Zine*; "just ice, when the fire's all done and lit" in *The London Reader's Raves & Resistance: Counterculture Stories*; "consent" in *The Medley*; "hasta ahorita" and "Leaving Leaving" in the world's oldest and most prestigious publication, *Instagram* and "fading out" in *Klang*.

Cheers, Tim Shelton-Jones, B; Mike Rehling, Kelly Sauvage Angel; Rebecca Robinson; Makis Moulos; James Diaz; Darren White, Carole Hill; Francis H Powell; Richard Ali, Wanjeri Gakuru; René Saldana; Matt Potter;

Dawn Bauling, Ronnie Goodyer; Sascha Engel; Areeb
Ahmad, Ira Patole, Shreyasi Banerjee, Aqdas Raza,
Damini Sarma, Kizhakoot Devika Babu; Cendrine
Marrouat, David Ellis; Jim Bennett, Patricia Hope;
Jannat Ahmed; Dan Knowles; Cailey Johanna Thiessen,
Maina Chen, Kiera S. Baron; David G. Walker, Beverly
Army Williams; Jade Elvina Hinder; Aisling Tempany;
DS Davidson; Adjei Agyei-Baah, Emmanuel Jessie
Kalusian; Shafinur Shafin; Janel Spencer, Lynn Finger;
Melanie White; Rebecca Buchanan; Whitney Smith;
Raamesh Gowri Raghavan; Heath Brougher; Maté Jarai,
'Stina Wilkins, Diletta Arzani; Michael Smith; Dagmara
K.; Robin White; Richard Gilbert, Clayton Beach;
Ashley Opheim; Kevin Carey, M.P. Carver; Karen Cline-
Tardiff; Vamika Sinha, Zoe Jane Patterson, Aathma
Nirmala Dious, Tusshara Nalakumar Srilatha, Sadaf
Habib; Troy Del Favero, Kaylin Kirk, Mary Sims, Daniel
Edmondson; James Reitter; Benn Ward; Robert Allen;
Susan Jane Sims; Geoffrey Gatza; Sam Smith; Ollie
Charles, Nicola Lampard; Gail Howard, Virginia
Howard; Taofeek Ayeyemi, Hemapriya Chellappan, Oni
Tomiwa; Nika Rose; Barry Spurr; Aimee Campos,
Monica Aleman, Jose Palacios, Adrian Kim Estrada,
Elissa Galadriel Faye, Laura Ingrid; Humphrey 'Huck'
Astley; Adrián Carrillo, Daniel Ardila; Fiorella Terrazas,
Karla Michelle Canett, Esteban López Arciga, Jesús de la
Garza; Lilith Pollock, Nathalie Götz; Núria Rovira
Terradas, Jenn Ashworth, Charlie Gere, Caty Flynn;
Briony Hughes, Saskia McCracken; Jonathan Penton;
Bryan Rickert, Don Baird, Stephen Bailey (Hansha Teki);
Jess Silfa; Holly Zijderveld, Lena Stein; Nikki Dudley,
Trini Decombe; Linda Gould; C. Cimmone; Hannah
Stone; Jasmin Perry; Amanda Marrero; Anatoly

Kudryavitsky; Juan Aguera; Haley Jenkins, Rebecca Shoulders, Katharine Cheetham, Stephanie Guerreiro Lourenço; Marzia Dessi; Jimmy E. Morales Roa, Andrea Duque; Santosh Kumar, Karunesh Kumar Agarwal; Darren J. Beaney, Barbara Mercer; Pepper Cunningham, Jacqueline Schaalje; Jide Badmus; Diana Mastrodomenico, Marco Costantini; Jason Wright, Chad Parenteau; Jim Lewis, Tricia Knoll; Joseph Fulkerson; Rachel Kendall; Jack Verschoyle, Bethany Brown, Léon Assaad, Matthias Albrecht, Zachary Stanley; Sonia Greenfield, Addy Robinson McCulloch, Jeri Theriault, Kai Coggin, Sorrah Edwards-Thro; Kala Ramesh; David L O'Nan; Mark A. Murphy; Cody Sexton; Carole Baldock; Katie McCann, Chloe Henderson; Marc Brimble, John Tessitore, Claire Thom, Mirjam Mahler; Meredith Grace Thompson; Michael Bartholomew-Biggs; Kate "Mary Fucking Poppins" Thomas; Diana May-Waldman and Mitchell Waldman, for liking my stuff before it was cool.

Floored

'spite

        tryin' our hardest

not to grow up

    to be

        alike

            our father

   's...

  we

a   'r

    in-

      articulate, fairly

     unattractive, unlike-

        able, misjudged

     by almost

           ev'ryone

    re: "Run,

       's,

    un-

     watched, over-

      looked, under-

    grounded

but deep down we

mean well

but deeper down we're
well mean

read us
go on
read us
n' weep

teacher throws away
incorrect haiku; with care
you uncrumple

"underaged"

                      under
                      under-
                                aged
                whisky
'␣s influence
␣s in-
    fluent fluent
  in
    glue n'
stuff sniffed, snuff
              's enough
              's enough dis-
                      still under
                      still   raging

To the thick of the forest

your black eyes
and your ears that do not yield
the right grain, they say
are too poor to enter
here, in this garden
party debate, underfed
by a mind malnourished
on peer-reviewed leaves, unbound
for HMS
Victory, unprinted
by the Oxford University
Press—a willow
is closer to Rousseau's
position on education as a marker
of social mobility
than to an oak
and it's high time you learnt

your place-
setting / at the bottom

of these woods.

Learner

I've pulled myself
free
of the wreckage
& now I'm ready
to climb
back behind the wheel.

footprints

long after   your death

we still follow
in the steps
you forgot
you   left
in the wet
cement

long dry.

I stop to check
and...   yep
exactly as I suspected
we're
different   sizes.

wrecking ball
begins its swing—
day-drinking

keep yr photos

keep yr photos
i remember how i felt
or
i dont

keep yr conversation
history
yr desk-top
table-talk
table
whiiine
ive got my
table mountain-top
hoooooooooooowl

keep yr himalayas
i cant even c m
frm up here

keep yr theories
n yr ideas
ive got my ecstasies
& my wild
animal
fears

keep yr souvenirs
ill always have my flashbacks
or
i wont

        take yr flash
back
    i have my fog

    keep yr herzog doc'
ive got the way
      yr fag ash exploded chinese dragon
breath on the tinted window
of that night

    keep my face
coz ive got trillions
    of yrs

    so keep yr photos

Go Faq yourself

after James Nicholls

Q: Why are you always drunk?
A: Reason.

The Queen of Heart

Her line
　　　　that goes nowhere
Her line
　　　　that couldn't be drawn straight
　　　　　　　with a ruler
Her divine right
　　　　　　to a pawn's moves, and
Her coronation
　　a corona bottle
　　to the face, and
Her castle
of broken glass
and sodd'n' (two
birthday)　card
Her Queen's speech
　　　　　　fractured
　　　　　　monotonous and
　　　　　　fowl
Her swans
　　　just ducks
　　　　　　with dirty arses
Her (pack of) hounds
　　　　a lone fox
Her portrait
　　　　in the gutter water
　　　as she stops
　　　　　　to pick up the penny
　　　　　　　at the very
　　　bottom

Her royal family
        of orphans
Her only servants
            her own hands
            her own legs
Her loyal subjects
    Society's rejects
Her suitors—
Our Queen in drag
        through
Her Grand
    Puke
            who watches her sleep
                        every night
                from the pillow beside—
                    its pillow case
                        of black
                            bin
                                liner

Her United Kingdom
                    of brain cells
                    of bloody-mind

Her crown
            of bald skin
    royally nuked—
    Her Thirty Years' War
            on Cancer
    Her jewels
        gnarls
                on cracked,
                    bare fingers
    Her guillotine
            that falls

                every day
                every minute
Her royal lowness
Her *Majesté*
The Queen of Heart
The only queen
        for me.

[Waste of space]

Worldview

there's a war in Ukraine;
thousands of homeless
line 5th & 6th
the guy from the soup kitchen appears
on the news
we watch
from Griffith Observatory
the city's enormous
plain of lights,
colored, flickers in the haze
everything is silent
everything is calm
from far enough away

haiking

the way
poorly signposted
→ war memorial

construction Work

kerouac before, cummings beforer

a poem prose
    railroad
        -ers, we mouthed you
            eared
                you'd
          beautifilled
       dress flowers perfumely
         —nose pur-for-Haitiens—
                pagans
          unbelievers
("No, t
      his time they're Xian
& white
& yellow & blue" he says, bide'n/"t
      his time
 it's not KO
Come?
 it's the opposite
ni NO")
                    in all probability,
noun-verb-adjectives—
               all humanity' S.
err-
          —or—

[Knock, knock!... Boom! Boom!]
     "Unclose

           down! It's Defective
Johnson¡„
     Unclothed
         & how!

        O how now

low hanging fruit

black bough
bent low to the ground—
storm clouds

Death in the city

They drove me to the stores
but didn't let me park

They fattened me up on Coca-Cola
but didn't let me in the bathroom

I suffocated on tailpipe fumes
and drowned in my own piss

They didn't provide a coffin.

songbird chick
thrown from the nest—
vow of silence

cockroaches find each other sexy

We,
frozen under the hot flood-
lights, in the dark fumble
for others who like us
strain to uphill get over
your mass, man-
made mounts of whipping
cream, disseminated
debris
and faecal matters
with which you auto-asphyxiate
every orifice, choke
every vent
of this bed
we share. Why
should it be you
and only you allowed
to breed
without contempt?

20/20s vision

after Chandra Livia Candiani

tired I's
of following / drastic
measures one-size-
fits-all / measurements undefined
blind-
folded   away
kidnapped milestones
in kilometres any way
all destinations turn right
RIGHT
THIS WAY
ONE-WAY DEAD-END
accelerating   fast
into a bend
blind-
moving goal-
posts / waving flag-white signs
walking upside-down
on our hands-
on / shifting   sands
STOP
spinning
GO
OPEN

no,
WAIT,
we're   CLOSED, mind
The Gap

seeing double
standards not standardised
laws not laid
down / rights not right
& all the while
doing right / by
rulers not straight
humans
inhumane.

The Towers of London

Run

Hermit
Field mouse
Caught

In bed

Of nails—
Stakes—

Towers
And estates
That grow
Like tumors
Out of the back of my hand
When there are no more fields

To run

undaunted gull
snaps the last crumbs—
receding land

escal(r)pe(ment)

Stopped by every escarpment.
Beaten by every thicket.
Moved on by every storm.
Forced to change course by every river.

but still,
    never still

the forgotten wordless
gunmetal argentine
back of a highway
roadside
sign
stilled against the wavering—destination
unknown

things to ban

for Joseph F. Glidden

there's no-one around
for hundreds of miles
but a spine and its ribs
hang
the wire that cuts divisive
the land—the next half-
swaddled in its former skin stiffened,
ripped away at
its edges—
the tattered *albiceleste* waving to no-one
never let
rest in peace
in the maddening Patagonia winds—the next
still has its eyes big beautiful
and dead—the next—
the next—every few yards
the next—until the one that still struggles
the one that could still be saved. But living
is the only state
never hang-
ing here on display (there's no-one around
for hundreds of miles). What
were they thinking
as they lost their last blood

to the desert shrubs
to the barbs
that protect
the absent owners'

land? There's no-one around
for hundreds of miles

the herd

licked
          enveloped—a stampede
                  powerful, but afraid
in numbers, of break ing   away
in moderation, moderately safe though

                                    for now

                  still prey

a great falling wave
your armchair at dusk,
landless bird

the search

I'm looking for someone brave
    but all my soulmates to be
keep falling
        to rare, tropical diseases;
    getting ~~cardiac~~

 arrested
    in the mid-
           dle of their dreams;
    jumping
       out of planes

 and hitting

 the Earth

 too hard

unnamed

the indiscernible tread
of communal footprints
stamped *en masse*
on the shores
of the Nyanza
they're still dredging
up new bones

locked soldier ants
throw their weight about
—silent disco

The Ballad of the Newsman

The Newsman cometh
　　　　　bleach white cloak
　　　　　　　　sound stomach
and colonically clean conscience.

　　　　The town's People
fuck all else to do, stand
　　　　needlessly handling themselves in the rain
eagerly anticipating
　　　　　　His coming.
Gather round children!
to hear what's new
　　　　what's relevant
and most importantly?
　　　　What's true.

Each a genius　　　　　　　　in his own eyes
　　　a fucking fuckwit in his neighbour's eyes
　　　　　　　they only have eyes
　　　　for the Newsman
　　　　　　　highly qualified, they're sure.
There's nothing but respect...
　　　　　...except?

　　　　The Rebel
thinks he sees spots:

            cold blood
        stains on the Newsman's cloak
                but all the People know
he's crazy
he's just a boy.

            The Governor
        his debts to the Newsman
locked away in The Cabinet
            filed under Re:gret
                with all the rest:
        hate mail
        black mail
        unflattering photographs
prefers instead a dirty bath
in his counting house
            counting all his expenses receipts
                wishing he had the Newsman's hairline.

                'The Invaders are in your very midst!'
                        The Newsman admits.

            The People   start having fits
        after paying him handsomely for his services.

        Meanwhile, the Rebel
catches a bad case of déjà vu
swears he's heard it all somewhere before
            this breaking news
                but all the People know
that's crazy
he's just a boy.

The Newsman speaks with confidence,
clarity
that unquestionable authority
they teach in Journalism School
in front of a mirror.

The Rebel has never seen a mirror.
He's always been quiet
and shy and
try as he might
fails to make himself understood.

'The Invaders cometh!'
The Newsman warns
his plastic crown of thorns
worn perfectly straight
every smile
laugh
and comma,

in its rightful place.

The People
Invaders themselves, just yesterday
sadly have Alzheimer's
and dementia,
are blind
partially deaf
and completely dumb.

They are Builders,   most
and builders fear most:

mass de-
struction

of their beautiful homes.
They build houses out of money
and, very occasionally,
          get money out of houses.

          The Rebel dreams of other rebels
                              in other towns, better
but suspects the Newsman has been ~~censoring~~ his letters,
                              with the latter's
          dove-feather pen.
                    But remember
he's crazy
he's just a boy.

          The Rebel appeals to the Book
          but the Newsman plays by the Book
                              for the Book
          even plays golf with the Book
on occasion.

'Eat dog or be eaten
     Kill or be killed
     Beat or be beaten'
               is the Wise-man's—
sorry,
               the Newsman's advice
as he slips out with his handsome pay
               just before the fight.

          So the People
          itching for the fun
               let bygones be—
                    buy guns

polish their guns
needlessly handle their guns
shooting slugs
and snails
too slow
small and frail
to put up a decent fight.

The Rebel suffers
sighing
in silence.
   That is, until people start dying
in silence.
He missed school the day they taught the meaning
of life, but
feels quite sure it's not to stand
idly by,   watch
                        and say nothing, while people
are dying
of ignorance
and violence.

If two-thousand People are wrong
and one lone Rebel is right
surely wrong must be right
and right must be wrong.

'Boy, there's nothing wrong
with needlessly handling yourself in the rain.'

The Governor hires Poppy.
                        Poppy appeals
to the People

who love her soft, rosy cheeks, all
        just
        to justify an Invasion
            on the Invaders.

        The Rebel
who sees her black, plastic heart
                burns Poppy.

            The People go from soppy
                    to ballistic.
            They love Poppy.
              Poppy
              knew their Grandma
            and they love their Grandma.

        How can the Rebel see a black heart
        when he finds it so impossibly hard
            to see Invaders from Invaders?
He's crazy.
He's just a boy.
 'Don't you know an Invader *when you see one, boy?'*

 He must've skipped school
the day they taught that too.

            Actually, just yesterday
                  (not too far back in time)
      Grandma gave the Newsman a piece of her mind
            stood up   and spat in his eye
          but the People sadly have Alzheimer's...

All that's left of Grandma is the Relic

                                                                     ধ

which the People polish with one hand
                              the other proudly waving
          to the Newsman.

          The Relic is a German porno mag
                              hard-core, of course
featuring pics of Grandma's fancy-dressed-up corpse,
                              MILFs and PAWGs
(and peppered with puppies
                    stuck in things)
          written by the Newsman
under his dove-feather pen name.

          The Rebel appeals
          to the Treasurer of the Social Club.
          He knows the Rebel's not crazy.
          He's connected
          but lazy

                                        and, besides,
the Social Club gets off on the smell of blood and lies
  and builds money out of clubhouses.

          So the Rebel attempts to assassinate
          the Newsman.
          So the Newsman says.
          Such a shame, say
          the Rebel's family and friends.
He's just a boy

                              but sadly the Book
just can't be bent.

          The Rebel is assassinated
                              by the Book.

'Scissors cut paper
  Rock beats scissors
Fear suffocates kindness
        causes blindness...'

            The Newsman, on his way to inform
                the Invaders
            (but which ones?)
                of the coming war
            make one last big score
        and feed his family of one
        (you were expecting 'four'?)
is accidently trampled to the floor
        by the coming Invaders.
        But which ones?
        Does it matter? He knew them both
In fact, he taught them everything they know.
                                Oh,
sorry,

                    you didn't know?

            The Newsman's handsome pay
scattered   worthless in the dust
            a yin-yang shaped battlefield
                just yesterday, a Builders' house.

            A tragedy!
            A crying shame!
The very thing they went to war to try to save!
There's cold blood on his cloak finely woven
of little white lies
            blood on his hands
            blood in his stool

                    ಕ3

and, in the sober light of day
just one of the People, after all.
                          His high qualifications, they're sure
are nowhere to be found.
Peace is restored
                    for now.

          Turns out wrong was wrong, after all
                          but the People sadly have
Alzheimer's...

Would You Pay A Rapist

your hard-
earned taxable gains
then pay them again
to watch the act? Then why
are you funding the mass,
non-consensual fucking
of millions of victims
then paying again
to watch the act?

becoming criminal

we let it slide
when you said we couldn't turn left
at that junction
and we couldn't turn right
we let it slide
when you picked us up for walking on the high-
way and again, for walking on the side-
walk. We let it slide when
you hit us
with a   fine. Fine,
we let it slide
when we got beaten
shitless and you stood idly by,
when you caught the thief
and offered us the once-in-a-life-
time chance to beat
him as he stood tied
helpless. We let it slide,
turned our eyes inside-blind
when you made our little sister cry
burnt tears,
blood, we let it slide
when you held our brother
by the throat
until he choked
out   and died.

                              We let it slide
                         when we finally tried
to make a sound but
                    you had each other's back   and lied.
                              We let it slide.
Even now   we let it slide.
                              But who am I
                                  to complain? I knew
                         your state of mind, I knew
                         your pre-cleared crimes
when I gave
you the job.

the ▮▮▮▮▮▮ law
▮▮▮▮▮▮ of the ▮
▮ wrong side ▮▮▮▮
the wrong ▮ of the law
the wrong ▮▮▮▮ law
the wrong ▮▮▮▮▮

৳৪

justice, when the fire's all done and lit

after Yusuf

If what they said
    was interesting
and their interests
    what they said

    I'd listen.

If their "rights"
    were right—
  their morals moral—
  their justice just

    I'd trust.

If their rules made sense
    and sense   ruled—
If their laws
      weren't so brok- en

    I wouldn't break 'em.

contempt of court

MINUTES
        faithfully put down
   second-
     guessed
The People v.
   persons
     of interest
   All rise...
please remain seated
[lets fall
the gavel
with the full
    downward
    force
  of the law]
 let's fell
the tree that grew
the gavel
  bring it all down
 sickle
and hammer
let nothing remain
of the bench but splinters
        How do you plead?
     It shouldn't come to that. But we will cry

out for death or exile   *(yours,*   *guiltily*
                                        of optimism,
                                          innocently
                                    of all malintent

You are hereby tried.
Well, at least we tried.
You are hereby held in contempt of court
                      hold me,
Your Lack of Honour,
                    you hold me
                              just
                                  right.

consent

for Nancy

They can beat me
imprison me
fine me
and sentence me to death.

But they can't punish me
without my consent.

For I'm a masochist
recluse
bankrupt
and suicidal.

Ha!

Hasta ahorita

My friends keep calling
to say I'm late, but
I'm only four
minutes
away

fading out

opening (bracket
(s) (in brackets)—footnotes[1]
in footnotes)—breaking
the spine within
the spine within
the spine within
the spine—sever-
ing
the connect-
shines to the brain—the memory
(of what I started out
to read (quickly)) quickly
fading...

[1] *in footnotes*[2]
[2] *in footnotes*

Leaving Leaving

There was a young man from West Leaving
Who learnt to control his own breathing
As soon as he'd clocked it
He immediately stopped it
And that was the end of his grieving.

March, 2020. The Limerick, Barcelona.

the morning dew
soon gone, beneath
our passing soles

Bacchus Against the Wall
—or— the orgy you know
damn well's coming

The Trans Oriental chugged
rolling into the station and we rolled
chugging onto the platform—'platform
O'—
me, my new mate the tourist, Lost,
and his cat, Uncastrated—in a golden shower, a deluge
of dirty plastic cups, crumpled beer cans and mountain
snow.

"Why you still hangin'
on-
to all that junk?"
I asked Lost
my mind
already bending t'wards thoughts o' lunch.

"For the memories, Dee"
he mumbled
as we stumbled up platform 'O'.
"Memories of what?"
"I don't remember just now. I just know."

Any baggage we might've had, we must've left
along the way:
a public bench? Down under
the cracked plastic table
of some backstreet *bar-café?*

Don't ask me again
where we've been
or why. Suffice to say
we've been to the extremes
of the earth or somewhere
over near that way.
"But...there's nowhere to go,"
I hear they say.
Well, we've been travelin' there,
anyway.

The Trans Oriental pulled out, left us
sodden,
ejaculated
a screech, in which I swore I heard all the major parts
of speech
say: "Doo, doooooo
your worst!"

We weren't surprised:
no-one there to meet us, to find
the station boarded up from outside

and felt it our duty
to bust this thing open
from inside.

I immediately rid myself of last season's antiquated
robes, brushed off the last of the mountain
snow, freefell as I shouldered my
bones, keeping just my socks on, for if I'm honest I was
still a little
cold. The tourist looked me up
and down, I looked at the cat
and the cat looked around.
"So?" "So what?" "What now?"

McDonald's seemed to be closed
"And how!"

We tried to hail a cab, but they were all smoking
burnt-out wrecks,
the drivers
cremated alive, the only thing untouched by the blaze:
their cigarettes.
"How sad," commented Lost.
"Oh? How so?"
"That smoking kills
and killing smokes."

You know, for a tourist,

he *was* an awfully witty bloke.

We tried to cross the bloody road,
but there were no more crossings
on these days,
all the lights had gone red
and looked like they were planning on staying that way
we had no choice but to jay-
walk this way and that. The cat
didn't give a flyin' shat:
had on his fur
inside-out, the label—well, everything—
just hanging out.
The best mind of his litter
fucking hysterical, dipping his brush-
like tail in *salvia* (sage) and dragging it dripping
through the streets gone grey
painting the town green—
this town on its knees—
as Lost yelled, "GO!" again and again
"Go where? Go when?"
"Just GO!" "But go where?" "I'm fucked
if I know!"

Well, you are most certainly fucked,
I thought.
He still wore
that straw hat with which they'd crowned our heads

at a dance... but *where?* it's easy to forget...
still had her nails
of considerable imperial length
(and don't even get me started on the girth)
pushed like animal horns into the corners
of his head, his shady
shades that he insisted he wore
to cover up the shame where
a black eye should've been—
his right eye socket
the only pocket on his entire body of unblemished skin.

Well, there's still time, I thought
but, to be honest, wasn't entirely sure...
one thing though *was* for sure: we'd better be quick,
"Come!"
I yelled. "I'm starting to get sick."

We made our way naked, wasted
through the wasted streets
towards the hill, our naked feet
unsullied on the peeling skin of
unshaved concrete
where the only jobs advertised
in the vacant eyes
of the carcasses
of the stores
were: "Volunteer policeman. No

need apply. The job's
already yours."
Oh, and of course:
"We want you
to keeping saying, 'Hey you! Stay indoors!'"
where the bars were "Open"
from three-fifty-four to five to four
under an equatorial twilight
gone grey, day-by-day
that's to say
unseasoned
without day, without night
the whir of 'copters
empty, without pilot
to the drone
of loudspeakers/
megaphones: recorded messages on repeat
no need
for real words anymore, just the senseless
bleat
of barnyard sheep.

We didn't come across a single soul.
But I guess that's nothing new
I don't know about you?

On the top of the hill
we stood like familiars

looking piteously down
upon the unfamiliar
familiar city, upon the desecrated Sagrada
Familia. "No.
It's supposed to look like that."
"Oh."

(Lost had his guidebook, you see
bent open wide three-hundred-and-sixty degrees:
All the best spots to get blitzed
to get high and
get down on one's knees. We tossed it off
over the güall:
where we were going, we weren't going
to need it. No,
not at all.)

Well, it was true:
all the restaurants were closed,
even *las hormigas* were starving—
an *hormigón* overdose.
"Luckily for us, Bee, the cat's got his nose."
(That was Lost, characteristically witty.)
So we followed the cat back down into the city.
"Good. With our nipples
exposed
like that, it was starting to get nippy."
So we followed the cat, who followed the reek

73

not of death
but of the opposite-of-living, back down into the streets
where emptiness reigned
and rains had emptied.

Lost tossed me his quizzical gaze
as we went right on past the courts
of law. I shrugged. "We're not here to make no case.
They've all been tried before."

With the exception of a pick-pocket, Redundant
and some out-of-work whores
the first follower
to rally to our cause
was a mute
drum kit we saw
poke her quivering finger
out of Doors
and come crashing, clashing
and splashing to our side.

Next came the bleached poster
of a two-year-old
drag show. "For me, it's only the dance
that matters, Lo'..."
With Uncastrated unrivalled
on the drums, we quickly won
the hearts of the young,

the old and the Royal Corpse
of the City Morgue—
both ends of the candle
burning brightest where closest
to the "nevermore"!

They led us to the home-
office of an easy-speakin'
monk, and there we got tanked
on his bathtub blood,
sweat and tears and mock-Trappiste swill.
"Jesus Christ!" Bawled Lost,
"He's actin' like a man
who's terminally ill!"
"You punks," chuckled the monk,
"you've got me pegged"
then proceeded to head-
bang his hair-free head.

From our new HQ,
together we found all the rebels
who'd all thought themselves
alone.
It wasn't difficult. It was almost all of you, you know?

We stood outside your houses
and watched you bathing
in artificial glow.

We took each individual
window and turned them on
one another, thrust
them up against
one another in an erotic kiss
until the glass broke
and doused us all
with sand, blood and the old, familiar feel
of unfamiliar flesh.

(We didn't have any problems communicating:
people'd got pretty used to talking to cats
so it was even a breeze for Uncastrated.)

Together
we made homeless the homeowners
tore down their wasted walls
that'd served for nothing, if just to cover their boners
and their private calls.

We dragged fifty-year-old homeschoolboysandgirls
from their mothers' aching teat.
We burnt the bra straps
that were holding up their sagging screens.
We cut the powerlines
that had them tied;
the fibre-optic cables
that had them strung up

and by the looks of it just in time.
We made glory holes of their gas masks,
we painted in any skin tone
over their mass-produced custom
designs,
whissssstled down the cavern-
ous wrinkles that had set up refuge-
e-camps around their
very eyes.

We pulled, we pulled
and we dragged
back the night
and we lit it on fire
with Fairy Street lights.

We pushed, we pushed
and we got the world re-turning
like the rollin' stone, baby
first sparking
then burning.

We marched,   rounding up
a homeless army
we marched
on the private parts, a public party
of '69
to the power of '69, rounding up—

"Halt! You're in violation...in breach
of the law: the prohibition
of gatherings
of more than one-
point-four!"

> *I'll give you violation*
> *I'll give you breach*
> *I'll give you a lesson in* our *law,*

I thought as Lost hissed,
"The fucking hypocrites! They're at least four score!"

"Stop this madness
        this instant!"

> *It's you who're mad.*
> *Only we can see.* I offered up my hands:
>   two low-fives—they slapped

the cuffs on me—they slipped
        off, with relative ease
"It seems
to be
some kind of grease!"
"We don't know anything
about where this guy's even been!"
"How can we get cuffs on his wrists
if we don't know even
one of his names?" They exclaimed.

"We know his hair's too long!
And his skin's too goddam pale!"

The reporters, joining via Zoom
took a collective shit.
"How we s'posed to spin our lies
without a thread of truth
to do it with?"

When they finally came
on us, the truncheons, they beat poor Lost within an
inch of his life—lucky bastard,
finally found that missing black eye—
yet from the ground
        he pointed out
for the truncheons a more fitting
application: we turned them on
themselves, turned them up their own arses,
hitherto clogged like a closet tight with toilet paper and
afterwards
they gushed
nothing but thank yous.
With the truncheons-
cum-dildos on side
that was all of us
unified.
There was no-one and nothing
to stop us

because we were *exactly* what you wanted
and nothing can stop you
doing *exactly* what you want.

We drank and smoked
ourselves like fish,
skipped royally 'round royally burning skips
rolled and tumbled and just for kicks
drew up a thesis on what might be
an ideal society's politics.

from libation to liberation furious frantic ranting raving
mad and the mad raving, a rebel revels as
rebels revel as reverberating bells, re: to berate (verb), ever-
present continuous: berating belles *"Balls!" "...some*
intense incense!" Incensed nonsensical nonsense: a
moaning slapping testical testimonial: bollocks, frollocks
defrocked, tried and tested untested, everything
and everyone
love-nested
arrested
and found inn*ocent*
aaand free...

old ladies once again
shared their needles
and the cats weren't the only cats
licking people

and once the fireworks and the orgy had plateaued—
found their home
in the very midst of our new way of life
Lost took off
his shady shades,
tipped me the straw
hat he still wore
with a tear in his eyes—
left, *and* right—
and said his goodbyes.
"I've got work in the mornin',"
he said and he sighed
and wandered off just as he'd come
into the last dregs
of the night.

And Uncastrated?
By his side?

Any cat there might've been,
we must've lost along the ride...
along the way...I seem to recall one cat dancing obscene
atop the table of some mainstreet bar-*café*...

ANXIETY PRESS

Printed by Amazon Italia Logistica S.r.l.
Torrazza Piemonte (TO), Italy